WORDSARONI

Word Play for You and Your Preschooler

by Linda Allison and Martha Weston

Little, Brown and Company

Boston   Toronto   London

The authors thank the moms, dads, aunts, uncles, teachers, librarians, and kids who generously shared their ideas, stories, and experience for this book.

A special thanks to Tracy Williams, Ethel Siderman, and the kids and staff at the Fairfax–San Anselmo Children's Center, Kathy Keswick, and the kids and staff at the San Anselmo Preschool, Betsy Partridge, Ann Pope, Barbara Young, and Joyce Hakansson.

A very special thanks to Patricia Monighan Nourot, Ph.D., Professor of Early Childhood Education at Sonoma State University, for guiding the content and adding her ideas, humor, and expert review.

Copyright © 1993 by The Yolla Bolly Press, Linda Allison, and Martha Weston

FIRST EDITION

10 9 8 7 6 5 4 3 2 1
WOR
Published simultaneously in Canada by Little, Brown & Company (Canada) Limited

The Brown Paper Preschool books are edited and prepared for publication at The Yolla Bolly Press, Covelo, California, under the supervision of James and Carolyn Robertson. Editorial and production staff: Renee Menge, Diana Fairbanks, and Alexandra Chappell. Composition by Wilsted & Taylor, Oakland.

LIBRARY OF CONGRESS CATALOGING-IN-PUBLICATION DATA

Allison, Linda.
   Wordsaroni : word play for you and your preschooler / by Linda Allison ; illustrated by Martha Weston. — 1st ed.
      p.   cm. — (A Brown paper preschool book)
   ISBN 0-316-03463-0
   1. Early childhood education—Activity programs—Handbooks, manuals, etc.   2. Language arts (Preschool)—Handbooks, manuals, etc.   3. Verbal behavior.   4. Interaction analysis in education.
   I. Weston, Martha, ill.   II. Title.   III. Series.
   LB1139.35.A37A43   1993
   372.6′1—dc20   93-2992

Printed in the United States of America

★ CONTENTS ★

★ ABOUT THIS BOOK ★

From the minute babies are born they are surrounded by a sea of language. Before they are a year old they begin making a babble language of their own. We call it baby talk, but your baby is trying very hard to make sounds that have meaning. Babies listen, they mimic, and soon they start saying words and stringing them together into sentences. Those first baby sounds turn to torrents of words and questions as kids begin to crack the communication code.

Should you teach your kids to talk? A silly question? Still many parents agonize about teaching their preschoolers to read. Why not gradually introduce your child to the pleasure of reading, the shapes of letters, the fun of making up a story? Little ones are eager to learn about everything, whether it's the sound of a bumble bee or the sound of the letter B.

We don't recommend pushing your preschooler to become a reader. But playing with language—learning words, saying rhymes, or having a daily storytime—will help your child to listen, to speak, and, eventually, to read and write, all in good time.

But *you* don't have time, do you? Anyone who spends time each day with a preschooler is busy by definition. That's why we wrote many activities in this book to fit those in-between times (like during a drive or on a trip to the store). Some of our suggestions take a bit of preparation, but the equipment is always simple. A short learning note begins every section. Read those when you do have a free moment. (You must have a few now and then.)

Research shows that surrounding your children with language and literature will inspire them to begin to read and write. Use this book as a guide as you explore the highways and byways of language and literacy with your child. But most of all have a good trip.

★ TALKING AND LISTENING ★

Tiny children do the magnificent. They transform themselves from babbling babies to walking, talking chatterboxes in a few short years. No one is sure exactly how they do this. We know they listen and mimic. But more is at work here.

Somehow they absorb the patterns and complicated rules of language. They know that one cat is called "cat" and more are "cats." Today they "go to the store," but yesterday they "goed to the store." (This sort of mistake shows that your child is learning the rules for past tense . . . and over-applying them.) Soon they'll say "went to the store," learning the exceptions as well.

Your child won't learn language skills at exactly the same speed as the kid next door. But chances are she will learn things in a similar sequence.

A baby loves sounds, his own and others', and he responds to his name and maybe his sister's and the dog's. By his first year he says words like "dada" and "mama," adding more at a rapid rate.

A two-year-old speaks in short sentences, asking questions like "Where kitty?" She can follow simple spoken instructions and delights in new words.

Your three-year-old knows 300 to 600 words, and he is beginning to understand concept words like big, up, and down. He asks why, when, and what questions in a steady stream.

Your four-year-old speaks in complete sentences. She can tell you what happened at Grandpa's yesterday and can follow spoken instructions with several steps. She asks even more questions.

By five most children can easily communicate ideas. They can listen to a story and answer questions about it. They may still mispronounce some sounds, but their speech is quite easily understood.

The activities in this chapter are designed to make talking and listening more fun and more fluent for you both.

★ SERENGETI SPAGHETTI ★

From the crib kids babble on just to listen to the music that their mouths make. Here's a listen and repeat game for sharpening the ears and limbering up the tongue. Say it soft. Say it loud. Get a rhythm going just for fun.

Play this game anywhere, anytime. All you need are some interesting words to say. No doubt you will collect your own.

Perfection is not the point. What's important is listening, talking, and having fun. Start with single words, and add on others for more challenge.

Hey, Eddy, wanna play Serengeti Spaghetti?

Okay.

Can you say spaghetti?

Spaghetti.

Right! Can you say Serengeti spaghetti?

Sperngeti sketti!

Okay!

Plant names, Italian foods, African towns, dinosaur names . . . great-to-say words are everywhere. Here are some fun words to try:

abracadabra	cucaracha
macaroni	humongous
bologna	mumble jumble
linguini	metacarpal
carpuzi	pterodactyl
cappuccino	timbuktu I love you
cucamonga	

Hey, Dad! Okefenokee!

FUNNY TALK

Change voices. Talk realllllllll slowwwwww. Use a deep, slow voice. Then try talking in a teeny, skinny, high voice. Play this as a variation with the Serengeti Spaghetti game, or all by itself.

★ WHAT'S ZAT? ★

Being able to listen and to identify sounds are basic survival skills. They are also basic steps toward learning language. Kids who have difficulty distinguishing one sound from another may have trouble saying and spelling words.

SOUND SURVEY. Shhh! How many sounds can you hear? Sit very still. Listen hard. Make a list together:

1. dog barking
2. hum of fridge
3. cough
4. rattle of newspaper
5. sound of cars
6. TV
7. skateboards on the sidewalk

(If you can't identify a sound, then describe it.) You'll be amazed at how many sounds you regularly blot out. Play this game anytime, anywhere.

NIGHTTIME NOISES. Sit with your child in the dark and listen to the noises in the night. It's a good activity for talking about scary things in the night.

SOUND EFFECTS. You will need a portable tape recorder for this activity. With your child, collect noises around the house. Play the tape back later. Can you identify all the sounds?

★ SIMON SEZ ★

Following instructions is something we do every day. Being able to hear clearly and to remember well are skills that develop slowly over time. Indeed, some of us are still trying to master them as adults.

You need two or more people. One person leads, and at least one person follows.

TO PLAY:

1. The leader says, I'm Simon and Simon says *(give an instruction)*:
- Clap your hands, turn around.
- Take one giant step, then say pahdiddle.
- Take a hop, a skip, then sit.
2. The follower listens and does exactly what Simon says.
3. Take turns being Simon.

Simon sez do this and then touch your toes with your tongue!

KNOW YOUR PLACE WORDS

Simon Sez is a good game for working with the vocabulary of space. Use these words in your commands:
- behind
- in front of
- on
- under
- over
- next to
- in
- around
- through
- beside
- near
- away from

HARDER. Challenge older kids with a longer series of things to do. Young ones may be able to handle only one instruction at a time.

CLASSIC SIMON. The rule is that the follower only does the command if the leader says, "Simon says." The object is to trip up the follower. At this point Simon and follower trade jobs. Only older kids will have developed enough ability to be able to both listen for "Simon says" and remember a number of instructions too.

★ SMALL TALK ★

Being a fulltime language coach comes with the territory of being a parent. It's exhausting. Sometimes it's too easy to slip into the "Uh-huh, that's nice, now quit it" mode of automatic response. Here are some hints for a better class of conversation with your young one.

- Putting thoughts into words forces kids to organize their thinking. It points out where understanding is muddy. Communicating what you know is as important a skill as knowing. Be patient; this skill takes a lifetime to develop.

- Respect what your kid has to say. Really listen, at least some of the time.

- Acknowledge his feelings. Instead of "Don't get mad," try "You sound very angry."

- Kids can wear you out with their millions of questions. Trim your answers to fit short attention spans.

- You may need to ask a question to find out what your child is really asking. "Why did the man fall?" might really mean "Did the man get hurt when he fell?"

- Ask your child open questions to get him or her thinking:
What do you think happened?
Why do you think the ice melts?
Do you remember when . . . ?

- But don't ask so many questions that your kid feels like he's always being quizzed. Kids need quiet and privacy too.

- A steady stream of "Don'ts" can sound like scolding. Instead of "Don't slam the door!" try "Can you think of a way to close the door more quietly?"

★ I SPY ★

A great game for in the car or while you're waiting for the dentist. Indoors and out, it's excellent for building vocabulary and sharpening everyone's powers of observation. Plus a whole gang of different aged folks can play.

Reading stories can also be a helpful way to connect with feelings. Sometimes it's easier to talk about people in books than in real life.

Reading aloud helps kids absorb some of the mechanics of reading. They learn that a page of squiggly lines has meaning, and those squiggles make words and tell stories. As they turn pages, kids learn that reading has a direction that flows from top to bottom, from left to right.

Books for babies? Definitely yes. Babies see colors and recognize shapes. They begin to connect spaces on the printed page with shapes and patterns in the real world. The beginning stages of pattern and word recognition take place very early, which is why it's never too soon to start with books.

Reading books can offer a calm, quiet time. And it's a fine time to snuggle up and be close to your kid. Reading a story can be a happy end-of-the-day ritual.

Reading can be a voyage of discovery. With books you and your child can meet dinosaurs or explore inside volcanoes.

Reading can introduce your child to new experiences like flying a plane or swimming underwater. Or it can allow you to prepare for an upcoming event, such as a trip to the dentist.

Most important, reading aloud lets you share the pleasure of books. Hopefully, it will be a pleasure that will inspire your child to a life-long love of reading.

★ STORYTIME ★

Kids who are read to early and often become early readers. One study found this to be true regardless of children's class, color, or IQ. There is a good chance that simply being exposed to ideas in printed form will help transform your child into a reader.

HINTS FOR READING ALOUD:
- Create a friendly place for reading.
- Introduce the book: "This book is about . . ."
- Read with expression.
- Link the stories you read to the experiences in your child's life. Listening to stories helps children make sense out of their world.

STORY TALKS
Let the tales you read open avenues of conversation. Ask questions that demand more than a yes or no answer. Accept your kid's response. Try to expand on it.
- What do you think will happen next?
- How do you think the dog feels?
- What would you do if you were in the story?
- How do you know he is sad?

PLAYING "BOOKS"
Encourage your preschooler to "read" to you or to her teddy bears. Playing with reading allows your kid to discover the social value and fun of literary activity, while trying out how it feels to be a reader.

★ PICK A WINNER ★

Don't expect your kid to love the same stories you do. He might find your favorite fairy tale boring, while adoring a story about the happy little truck you find so tiresome. Try a range of books to discover your child's favorites.

Choosing for age. For preschoolers of any age, pick sturdy books of a size that is easy for small hands to handle.

- BABY BOOKS (infant to one)
Pick books that can take being chewed and battered. Washable books are best.

- TODDLER BOOKS (one to three)
Few words, big pictures, and lots of page turning make the most successful books for this age group.

- PRESCHOOLERS (three to six)
As your kid's attention span lengthens, choose stories that are longer and more complex.

- Pick books you like. If you can't get enthusiastic about reading, your child won't either.

- Pick books with interesting language. Rhythm and rhyme are a joy to read.

- Don't avoid new words. Learning a new word by hearing it used in context is a basic skill.

- Retire books temporarily. If you can't stand to read that stupid book about trucks one more time, be honest. "I'm really tired of that book. Please choose another."

Library Time. When asked how young a child she liked to see in her library, our favorite librarian said, "It depends. I've enjoyed some as young as two. Then again . . ." Some young ones mostly enjoy pulling great piles of books off the shelves. Willy's mom waited until he became more interested in what was inside books, at about age four. Then trips to the library became part of his routine.

Dory's librarian was sympathetic. "We have a lot of three-year-olds who like to reshelve the books." She was happy to help Dory's mom find books of interest. Whatever your situation, don't pass up the storytimes, videos, and books. Once children get the hang of it, libraries can be magical places for them.

Okay, I'll read your book about the slug if you listen to this new one first.

★ BEGIN WITH A BOOK ★

Look to books as the starting places for other activities. Charley is crazy about dinosaur books. One day he decided to make a dinosaur museum in the hall with his personal rubber reptile collection. His family all came to visit. Next time he thinks they might need tickets.

Goldilocks and the Three Bears could start a discovery session about papa-, mama-, and baby-sized cups, shoes, and chairs.

Jack and the Beanstalk is the perfect excuse for planting a couple of beans in a paper cup and watching them sprout.

Little Red Riding Hood might be an inspiration for packing a picnic basket for a wolf-free trip to grandmother's house. If she is too far away, make a drawing of a picnic and send it to her.

I'm giving her lots of bananas and gum.

(Label each item.)

Make a Play. For a dramatic change, try acting out a story instead of flipping on the TV. "There were three little pigs. OK, the kids and Dad are the pigs, and Mom's the wolf." Any quick props you can find will make the play more fun.

Not by the hair of my chinny-chin-chin!

Over and Over
"My kids throw a fit if I read a story they know and I leave out ONE word. They want to hear the same story over and over again. It's *so* boring." Boring for adults, but little children love repetition. Repetition allows them to really absorb a story. It helps them anticipate and predict what will happen next. Think about it. Small children live in a big, scary, and unpredictable world. Repetition helps them feel powerful and safe.

Book Review. Retell a favorite story together. Nurture your child's language skills by talking about books. "What happened to Puss first? Then what happened?" and so on.

★ TELLING STORIES AND MAKING SENSE ★

People around the world tell stories of heroes, of villains, of the events of their lives, and the lives of their kin.

Telling stories is a way of telling about ourselves, our world, our hopes, our fears, and our dreams. A story is a place to tell about ideas and feelings. Stories put us in touch with family and friends, our future and past.

Stories tell us how to act and how not to act. Stories let us make up fantastic worlds and, *boom*, destroy them with a single word. Stories take us to faraway places and places deep inside ourselves.

Stories are a way of connecting with the people in your circle. Making a story is a way to make sense out of the world.

Our modern world, with its barrage of messages, movies, and news, makes listeners out of us all. We hear many stories, but we tell few of our own.

Speak up! You have your own special tales to tell. Share them with your child and, together, make time to tell those special stories that you share.

★ TELLING TALES ★

Storytelling is an activity that requires extended thinking. A storyteller must remember where he's been and think ahead to where he's going. This is a lot for a little one to hold in his mind. Expect to do a lot of filling in. But that's the beauty of a back-and-forth tale.

GRAB BAG TALES. Storytelling can be the perfect activity for anyplace you have to wait. All you need is a purseful or pocketful of things to use as props.

Begin the tale: "Once upon a time there was a magic . . ." Let your child reach into your pocket or purse and pull out a magic . . . paper clip.

Continue the story: "The paper clip was magic because . . ." (Use your imagination and the props to weave the wildest tale you and your child can think of.)

STORIES TAKE PRACTICE
Don't expect either you or your child to spout off nonstop stories at first. Telling stories, like everything else, is a skill that is learned. Stories have a shape. They have characters, a place, and a pace. Take your time. You and your child will gradually get into the rhythm of telling tales.

The foolish pencil was lonely way out there on Jupiter. He needed a friend.

Here is his friend... a bagel! But someone tooked a bite out of it...

ONGOING TALE. One mom describes storytelling with her four-year-old this way: "Simon and I started telling stories, and now we seem to have an ongoing adventure. Simon always begins the adventure by going through a tunnel and coming out in another world. The same characters stay in this story, although new ones are added in as the story grows. It's a lifesaver for those in-between times."

Now, where were we? Mr. Frog had the flu?

Yeah.. And he was so sick he had to take ...

Oh, no! Captain Hook is coming back! No, wait, he's gone under again!

STORIES TO DISTRACTION

Parents are cunning folks, trying anything to get their way. "The way I get Ben's hair washed is to play Captain Hook. I say that Hook hates having his hair washed, so Ben rubs his Hook doll all over with shampoo. Meanwhile I suds up Ben's hair while he drowns Hook over and over. Before you know it we're done."

A dog found a skunk.

Fortunately the skunk was asleep.

Unfortunately the skunk had a daddy and he was awake!

FORTUNATELY, UNFORTUNATELY

Adding lines to a story one at a time is an interesting way to spin a yarn. Here's a way to tell an alternating tale with a twist. One person starts:

"Once there was a princess who only ate purple foods. *Fortunately* her garden was full of eggplants and berries."

The next person adds a line beginning: "*Unfortunately* she couldn't stop eating them. Which made her very fat."

The next person begins: "*Fortunately* fat princesses were much in demand."

The tale goes on until someone finishes it—fortunately.

...and then she spit out the squash and said, "Yuck!"

TODAY'S TALE. Instead of reading a bed-time story, make a tale out of the events of the day. Make your child the main character:

"Today Esmeralda began the day when she *woke up in a grumpy mood*. First she *went for a walk with Nana*. And then she *ate ice cream for lunch*. Next she *played with Rufus the rat, watched TV, ate dinner, and spilled her milk*. And then she *crawled into bed, and her dad tucked her in, gave her a kiss, and said good night. Esmeralda gently floated off to dreamland*."

★ FINGER PUPPETS AND HAND FRIENDS ★

Kids move effortlessly from the real world to fantasy and back again. Pretend play offers children a safe place to try on new roles, to act out ideas, and to rehearse for real life. Finger Puppets and Hand Friends are always close by—all you need is a pen to draw them out for a little instant theater.

FINGER PUPPETS. Finger puppets can be ready in a flash. Just draw them directly onto your finger. Use a thin felt marker. First draw the lips on the crease. Then add eyes and hair.

"Do you want a boy or girl?"
"How about some hair?"
"OK, I'll put in a mustache."

Wiggle your finger to make him talk.

GLOVE PEOPLE. Snip off the finger of a solid-colored glove. Draw features on it with a contrasting pen. Glue on hair and accessories, if you like.

HAND FRIEND. Make a fist with your thumb inside. Pretend your wrist is the neck. Draw on lips and eyes with a marker or makeup pencils. Wiggle your thumb to make your Hand Friend talk.

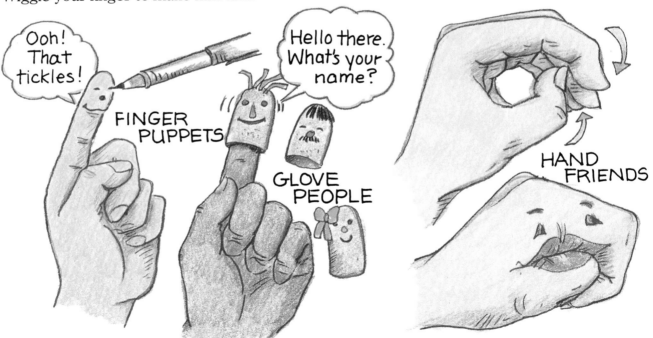

Children are often suddenly shy around a new person. Finger people may be no exception. Playing puppets with your child will gently introduce many elements of storytelling and theater.

SET UP A STAGE on the edge of a table and get right down into the world of your finger people. Explore how finger people walk. Where do they go when they are sleepy? Where do they live? What do they do when they are bad? Revisit your finger people soon. You'll find that they will have more to say the next time around.

HINT: Puppets make a great audience. Let your child take them on a literary excursion as they "read" them their favorite book or tell them a story.

TALKING WITH FRIENDS

Ben really likes his Hand Friends. His mom says, "We don't bother to draw eyes and lips on them, though some people do, so these instant hand puppets are always close by. Ours are really affectionate, kissy creatures. Ben will say things to a Hand Friend that he won't tell me. Somehow, to him, Hand Friends are real."

★ LEARNING WORDS ★

Some of those meanings are straight-forward. For example *cat* means fuzzy animal that scratches. *Noodle* is the name for a long, slippery food. But some words, like the word *heavy*, aren't so easy to understand. A lot of different things can be heavy. A lot of different things are called *red*. And a lot of things are called *danger*.

Kids do an astounding job of absorbing words. In the first year most babies will learn a few first words. By six a kid's vocabulary will shoot to 1,500 words. That's enough vocabulary to get along in a foreign country, and more than enough for a child to express almost anything he or she needs to say.

But learning to talk is a lot more than simply learning words. Babies must learn to coordinate their breathing and mouth muscles to reproduce the sounds that they hear. Then they must put these sounds together in ways that make sense to the big people in their world. Besides mastering their new equipment, kids are learning the meanings and ideas behind every word.

Every word is a tool that represents things and ideas and has the power to communicate those ideas to others. Understanding words helps unlock ideas about how the world works. Make sure you help your kid get all the words she needs.

★ NAME GAME ★

Everything has a name. And there is a special set of squiggles (called writing) for showing the name of something on paper. Amazing. Explore some new words together, write them on labels, and "read" them as you stick them onto the real, live thing.

You will need:

masking tape or sticky notes
a marker

TO PLAY:

1. Body parts are a good place to start. Point to something. "What do you call this?"
2. With your child's prompting, write the word *nose*. Then stick it where it goes.
3. Label your way around the body.
4. Play the Name Game in the kitchen, the bathroom, the car, outdoors, or in the garage. Label your kid's drawings, paintings, or building-block sculptures.

HINT: Leave the notes in place for your child to "read" later, or collect them all for another day.

BAD WORDS

You know the ones, body parts and bathroom talk. Why do such adorable children insist on using such awful words? Simple. They get a big reaction. The more reaction they get, the more fun they are to use. Forbidding these powerful words only gives them more appeal. Smart adults let a child know these are words that most people don't like to hear. In a neutral tone, without fuss say, "You can use those words in your room, but I don't want to hear them." In the case of swearing you might suggest alternatives. Say, "I don't want to hear that, but it's OK to say dunderhead, bean brain, or oh shoot!"

★ ACT OUT WORDS ★

A teacher once described adults as people who learn from the neck up and children as people who learn from the neck down. Children naturally love learning things with their whole bodies—words are no exception. This one word version of charades is a fun way to communicate without talking.

1. With your child, decide on a category such as animals or foods. Pick a word. Act it out so that another person can guess what it is.

2. Try using simple action words that your child knows, then move onto other categories. Choose whatever is fun to act out.

ACTION WORDS: jump, skip, turn, fall, wiggle, clap, crawl, hop, sneeze.

POSITION WORDS: inside, on, under, around, through, out, over, outside.

FEELINGS: happy, sad, scary, grumpy, sleepy, furious, cranky, silly, crazy.

ANIMALS: dog, cat, bunny, grasshopper.

FOODS: spaghetti, Jell-O, banana, honey.

EASIER. Younger children will have an easier time acting out things with sound effects: a motorcycle, fire engine, dog, cat, vacuum cleaner, telephone.

HARDER. Act out a whole sentence: "The dog ate the flower."

★ MY WORD BOX ★

One day it dawned on Sylvia Ashton Warner, a teacher of Maori children in New Zealand, that kids would learn to read faster if they were reading words they got excited about. She invited her students to pick their own "key words," and they began reading with phenomenal success.

1. Ask your kid to tell you his favorite words. Pick powerful words that your child is attracted to.

2. Write them on cards. Color them. Say them together. Add a picture if you like.

3. Keep them in a special box. Take them out often and say them together. Soon your child will read them on his own.

This is my best word — tyrannosaurus.

Hint: Some kids like to wear their words clipped to their belts for handy reading.

PINKLE

Felix was fascinated with colors. By the time he was two, his mom says he could name ten. "Hey, Felix, what color's this?" she asked, handing him a lavender scarf. He struggled with this new hue, and after a tortured minute he blurted out, "Pinkle." Not only was it a great word, but a great moment watching Felix master the logic of language.

These wondrous words are often so vivid, and they become part of the family lore, but many are lost. Make your own word box for saving them. These word gems are too precious to lose.

screw-babba

metermeiser

Kitty is betowards me.

Mommy, the sun is brighting me!

★ SIGNS OF LIFE ★

Streets are full of words, some of which are important to know. Give your kid an introduction to street smarts and sign reading with this card game. Anytime you hit the streets for a walk or a ride is another chance to read signs together. Soon your kid will be reading signs on his own.

You will need:
3×5 cards, cut in half
markers or crayons

1. Draw or copy the pictures on this page onto cards. Keep one side blank.
2. Make two of each card.
3. Color the cards, if you like.

TO PLAY:
1. Shuffle the cards. Deal them out in rows, face down.
2. The first player turns any two cards face up.
3. If a match is made, the player keeps the pair and takes another turn.
4. If not, the cards are turned face down again and the next player tries to make a match.

I matched!

PICTURE CONCENTRATION
Make Concentration cards with any matching pictures. Cut these from two issues of the same magazine. Animals, colors, desserts, and toys are fun cards to play.

Two dogs!

★ DOOHICKEY ★

Many times you can learn a new word by figuring out how it is used in a sentence. It's never too soon to learn this important skill of context for discovering meaning. Here's a silly game for some serious practice with context. Sometimes this game's called Teapot, but use any word you fancy.

TO PLAY:

"That darned *doohickey* barked all night. What is the *doohickey*?"

"A duck."

"No, silly. I'll give you a hint: the *doohickey* barks, and the *doohickey* has fleas."

"Oh, I know . . . *doohickey's* a cat."

"Do cats bark?"

"I mean a dog."

"Hey, Jenny. My *teapot* jumped into my lap, and the *teapot* purrs whenever I pet him. Guess what the *teapot* is."

"Jana *gizmoed* the book, then she *gizmoed* the newspaper, and *gizmoed* a story until she fell asleep."

Dad! Dad! Look out!

A bumbly?

Der's dis huge bumbly on your foot! And — dis is <u>so</u> bad — der is bumblies all over de floor in your closet and der is one under your bed!

TODDLER HUMOR

Little ones love the absurd whether it's with words or actions. For instance, putting two socks on one foot can be great fun for a three- or four-year-old. What the child's saying is "I know the real way to do that, and I can deliberately not do it, which makes me incredibly powerful . . . and funny."

By the end of his first year, your child will probably stop sucking his crayons, and he will discover the fun of scribbling marks across a paper, a wall, or anything at all.

To make marks is as natural as the urge to speak. Those random scribbles soon take direction and shape as your child learns to control his marks.

Around the age of three a child begins to draw simple shapes. During the next year most children begin to tackle writing their name and drawing recognizable pictures.

Gradually children begin to use combinations of letters, scribbles, and pictures to carry their messages in a kind of writing of their own creation.

At about kindergarten age they begin making words and inventing their own spellings, eventually moving toward conventional spellings.

Learning to write is a process with many steps. Don't rush your child. Enjoy the process as it unfolds. As you wipe the crayon marks off the walls, take comfort in the fact that even the greatest writers began their careers by making scribbles.

★ THE WRITE PLACE ★

It may look like chicken scratches to you, but your child's early writing deserves your encouragement. You can encourage your child by providing easy access to writing tools and lots of your enthusiasm.

WRITING PLACE. A writing corner may encourage your kid to do her writing in the "write place" and not on her bedroom wall. It might include:

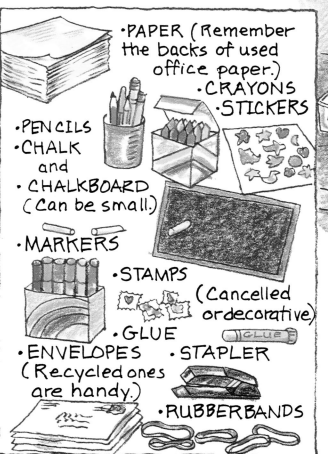

- PAPER (Remember the backs of used office paper.)
- CRAYONS
- STICKERS
- PENCILS
- CHALK and
- CHALKBOARD (Can be small.)
- MARKERS
- STAMPS (Cancelled or decorative)
- GLUE
- ENVELOPES (Recycled ones are handy.)
- STAPLER
- RUBBERBANDS

Kids write in a number of ways, including scribble writing, random strings of letters, picture writing, and invented spelling. These are your child's creative experiments as she works to crack the complicated code of reading and writing. Encourage your child to write as she likes.

HINT: An old typewriter has great appeal. Little ones feel very accomplished tapping out row and rows of letters.

★ WRITE ALONG ★

Making a shopping list? Dashing off a birthday card to Auntie Em? Updating a phone list? Perhaps your child would like to sign the card or make his own list (in his own writing, of course). Mail those letters. Take those lists along to the grocery store. Later ask him to read what he wrote. Treat your kid's writing with respect to show him that his writing efforts are important.

PHONE LIST. Write the names of all the important people you call. Next to their names, list their numbers. Don't forget 911.

SIGNS. This sign started out as a shirt board. It later appeared on a four-year-old's door. Look closely. It spells "Keep out. I say keep out."

SHOPPING LIST. Perhaps your child has some special things he would like to pick up at the market. Make your lists and take both along to the store.

CARD. To make a birthday card, fold a stiff sheet of paper in half. Have your child draw a picture on the front, then "write" a message inside.

★ CAPTIONS ★

Writing down your child's words lets him know what he has to say is important. Changing spoken words to written words shows your kid that print carries meaning. Plus it's a wonderful record of whatever you're doing at the moment. Save some of those moments in a scrapbook.

DICTATION. When your child finishes a drawing, ask what she drew. "Tell me about your picture. Do you want me to write down what you said underneath?"

Later, ask her to "read" you her picture. Or read her words back to her.

MAGAZINE STORY. Have your child choose a magazine picture that appeals to her. Invite her to "write" a story about the picture, using any words she likes. Have your child "read" it back later.

HINT: Write your child's *exact* words. This allows her to see her own words translated to print and to hear them again later.

★ PRINTING WORDS ★

Older preschool children may be eager to try writing words "right." Letters don't need to be introduced in any order. Start with any word your child chooses. Odds are it will be his name. If you find yourself getting frustrated with your kid's slow progress, try using your other hand to remind yourself how awkward it feels to learn how to write.

1. Let your child choose a word. Write it on a card in bold block letters. (It's best to stick with capital letters to begin with.)

Give him a soft pencil and a big sheet of paper.

Here's LYLE. This is how you write it.

It starts with the letter L. Then the letter Y. Looks like a man with his arms up. Look, another L. And last, the letter E.

Do you want to try it?

2. It might help to pick up your child's finger and slowly trace the letters as you talk about their shapes.

3. If your child gets frustrated, try one letter at a time. Or try tracing or connect-the-dots writing as a way of getting started. Sometimes drawing letters in the air is helpful practice.

HINT: Sometimes your kid will be intensely interested in an activity like writing. Then, for no reason you can see, he abandons it for days or even weeks. Don't push. Allow him to move at his own pace.

TRACING. This can be a really satisfying way to begin to make letter shapes. Write some bold letters with a dark line so they're easy to trace. Have your child trace them with a grease pencil on clear plastic or see-through paper. Plastic erases easily with a paper towel.

CONNECT THE DOTS. Make a dot pattern of the letters of the word. Put the dots close together. Let your kid connect them with a pencil line.

WRITING "RIGHT"

Does your kid just scribble? Look closer. This is writing three-year-old style. Simply holding a pencil is a big job for a small kid. Learning muscle control to get the pencil where she wants it to go is hard work. Writing also requires mastery of a whole world of symbols and forms that must be assembled in order to make sense. The conventions of the page, reading top to bottom and left to right, must also be learned. Don't belittle your child's first scrawling attempts. Learning to write "right" is a big job, and kids need all the encouragement they can get.

Children begin to write with scribbles as they learn to control the pencil.

Soon the marks begin to take direction and shape.

Kids begin to show "word sense." They begin to relate letters to sounds, inventing their own words and spellings.

Learning the alphabet is a little like meeting 26 new faces and trying to remember all their names. It's a big job. Introduce your child to just a few letters to begin with, in any order that feels right. Why not start with the letters that spell your child's name? Use letter blocks, or cards, or simply write your kid's name in block letters.

"Iris, let's make your name. The first letter is I. It's tall and straight and it looks like a stick of gum."

Talk about how the letters look. How are they alike and different? What overall shapes do they make?

"Next is R. It's a straight line with a bump on it, and another short line.

"Oh, look. Here's the letter I again. Your names has two Is.

"And the last letter is S. It looks curvy like a worm." (Encourage your kid to make his or her own associations.)

Introduce new letters to your child when he or she is ready for more. Work with the capital letters first. Later, when your child easily recognizes most letter shapes, introduce the lowercase letters.

TRY ACTING OUT LETTERS...

Look at me. I'm a T!

Hey, Mom, Billy next to Puff makes letter

Can you be an S?

Sure!

★ ALPHABET SOUP ★

Pick a letter of the day and watch out! This letter lurks everywhere, just waiting to be identified. You'll find it turning up on cereal boxes, in the street, on the dog's license, written on your T-shirt. Here are a few letter identification games to play.

HEADLINES. Cut out a handful of newspaper headlines. Pick a letter, S for instance. Give your child a crayon and see how many times she can find and circle the letter.

ALPHABET SOUP. Always a treat, but we don't eat the Ps. Not today. No way. Because these are the letters we're looking for.

LURKING LETTERS. There are plenty of places to find the letter of the day. Look for it:
- on labels in the store or on your shelves
- on street signs
- in magazines in the waiting room
- written on your shoes

> Oops! I eated a P!

> Mama, buy that! It has one, two Fs on it.

> Fran's Fiery Salsa?

ALPHABET BOOKS

Illustrators often do their best work in alphabet books. Check out a few of these beauties at your library or bookstore. Bring one home, settle down in a cozy spot with your child, and step into a colorful world of letters and sounds.

★ ICEBOX ALPHABET ★

Magnetic letters are a great invention. Letters and the fridge are a team that naturally clicks, allowing your child to play all sorts of alphabet activities while you're busy in the kitchen. Since they're cheap, why not buy a couple of sets?

MATCH ME. Spell out a word with letters. How about *fish*? Can you find the matching letters to make *fish*? Take turns and let your child spell a nonsense word for you to match.

SING THE ALPHABET SONG. Put up the letters in order as you go along.

SOUNDS LIKE. Banana, bum, brat, bagel, broccoli, bugs. . . . Find the letter that makes the bbbb sound.

NAME IT AND YOU CAN HAVE IT. Slide all the letters over to one corner. Pull the letters out one by one. "Name it and you can keep it. If not, I get it." Try a color variation: "Can you find all the red Os?"

All these activities can be done with letters printed on cards, but cards don't do as good a job of hanging around as magnetic letters. P.S. Magnetic letters are a colorful way for the whole family to leave messages long past preschool.

★ DOUGH Ds AND PANCAKE Ps ★

To make a letter a kid really has to slow down and study a letter's shape. Here are some crazy ways to make letters. Some of them are good enough to eat! And they will all help your kid absorb the shapes of letters.

DOUGH LETTERS. Roll a batch of refrigerator cookie dough into ropes. Form the ropes into your favorite letters on a cookie sheet. (If you need a guide, scratch block letters on sheets of aluminum foil and form the letters on the foil.) Bake and eat.

Try this with clay or playdough. (Skip the eating part.)

foil

PANCAKE LETTERS. Thin pancake batter can be formed into letters on a grill. Do this with a turkey baster or a squeeze bottle. Munch those letters for brunch.

PUDDING PLATES. Spread a thin layer of instant pudding onto a plate. Draw letters in it with your finger. Lick your writer clean. Yum!

SIDEWALK SCRAWL. On a warm day, draw letters on a sidewalk with an ice cube. On a hot day, you will have to write fast, before the letters evaporate into thin air.

It's freezy!

★ NOODLE NAMES ★

Picking out noodle letters to make your name is fun. Making them into a bracelet is even more fun. Buy a bag of pasta letters or alphabet cereal at the market. Do those little fingers a favor; buy the biggest ones you can find.

You will need:
a bowl full of pasta or cereal letters
a thin sheet of colored cardboard or plastic
string
a paper punch
white glue

4. Squirt a thin line of glue onto the cardboard. Invite your child to stick the letters on in order.

5. When the glue dries clear, tie strings through the holes and put on the bracelet.

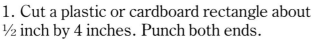

1. Cut a plastic or cardboard rectangle about ½ inch by 4 inches. Punch both ends.

2. Pour a handful of cereal or pasta letters onto a colored plate. Ask your child, "Can you find the letters to make your name?"

3. If your child needs help, print her name on a card and see if she can pick out the correct letters. Or pick them out for her and invite her to put them in the right order by matching them.

★ MY B BOOK ★

Letter books are a great way to learn beginning letter sounds. Add words under the pictures. They make nifty little dictionaries. Later, take them apart and shuffle them for some colorful sorting games.

You will need:
magazines to cut up
3 × 5 cards
scissors, glue stick, paper punch
rings (from a stationery store)

5. Add to the B Book anytime. Meanwhile you might start a D or a P Book.

HINT: It's best to start with letters that "say" their name like B, T, P, R, M, and S. Letters like H, Y, and W can be confusing.

1. Pick a letter. "OK, B."

2. Together, look through magazines and find pictures that begin with the letter B. "The letter B sounds like bees, beans, bikes, beeble, berries. . . ."

3. Cut out a handful of pictures. Glue each picture on a card and print its name under the picture.

4. Punch the corner of each card with a hole. Slide the cards onto the ring and close it.

WHAT SORT?
- Shuffle cards together from books of different letters. Sort the Bs from the Cs and the Zs.
- Sort them by category. Try animals, machines, foods, or whatever seems to fit.
- Sort them by big and little.
- Sort out the things you can eat from things you can't eat.
- Sort the things you like from those you don't like.
- Make two stacks, one of things with feet and one of things with no feet.

★ RHYME TIME ★

Fool. Cool. Rum. Dum. Doodle. Poodle. Kit and Caboodle. Rhymes are irresistible to say and a good way to practice the sounds that letters make. Playing with groups of rhyming words or word families will make it easier for a child to recognize word families when he begins to read later on.

RHYME TIME. Start the game with any rhyming sentences:

- A fat cat sat on the mat and squashed my hat.
- The fool in the pool is too cool!

Eeny, meeny cho cha leeny, I buy gumbaleeny. Achee, pachee, liverachee, Out goes you!

Rhyme Time! Mop...

Bebop!

Mama...

Llama.

When your kid has heard a few rhyming lines, announce the game: "Rhyme Time. I say *hat*. You say ——." (Your child fills in with a rhyme.)

After your child learns to play, pick up the game anytime. Say, "Rhyme Time," and you're off.
"Silly . . ."
". . . Willy."

SECRET SOURCE

Kids' rhymes have a whimsy and vitality that appeal no matter how old you are. Ask your librarian for books of jump rope rhymes or children's lore.

DON'T STOP. Go beyond one-word rhymes. Memorize verses you like. Teach them to your child. Recite the rhymes you know. Remember those old jump rope ditties, jingles, and snippets of poems. Oh, yes! You know the ones.

NOT RHYMES

1. Spout off a list of rhyming words, for instance, "sox, lox, dox, rox, moo, mox."
2. Ask your child, "Listen, Liz, which word doesn't rhyme?" (Liz needs to listen closely to pick out the nonrhyming word.) "Having trouble? OK, I'll repeat it."

CHANTS, RANTS, ELEPHANTS!

Pick a word, any word, and fool around with it by changing its beginning sound. This goofy game is fun to play anywhere, anytime (lime, dime). Plus it's a fun way to practice rhymes.

1. "Hey, Jason, pick a word."
"OK . . . *dumb*."
2. Together or alternately, change the first letter of dumb to change the word. "Bum, rum, sum, lum, zum. . . ." (The words don't have to make sense.)
3. Try making the words into a singsong and have fun chanting the list back as fast as you can.

RHYME TIME WORDS

Here are some rhyming words to get you started:

- back, rack, jack, hack, lack, pack . . .
- bake, cake, lake, take, sake, make . . .
- am, ram, bam, lamb, sam, cram . . .
- art, smart, chart, heart, dart, tart . . .
- ice, dice, mice, rice, lice, nice . . .
- big, pig, dig, rig, jig, fig, gig, twig . . .
- pop, bop, mop, cop, stop, hop, whop . . .
- ale, tale, sale, pail, hail, jail, mail . . .
- ate, bait, crate, date, mate, late, nate . . .

Whether you're a sworn enemy of TV, video and computer games, or a happy couch potato, you can bet electronic media is not going away. If anything its effect on our lives seems to grow each year. It began with radio, increased with TV, and gained ground with the VCR. Computer and video games are promising to expand into "Virtual Reality," a wrap-around electronic simulation that some say will be more exciting than real life.

Whether or not electronic entertainment turns out to be more interesting than real life isn't the issue. Right now the media occupies a big space in most of our lives. (The average American watches about 28 hours of TV a week starting at the age of two.)

For young ones the line between what's real and not real is often fuzzy. Everything they see on TV seems real to them. This makes small children especially vulnerable to TV, video, or any electronic programming. Kids need an adult to guide them away from what's too scary or confusing for them to absorb. And they need help interpreting what they do see.

Still, hardly anyone would choose to live in a world without media because it enriches our lives in many ways. The trick is to know how to use it to open doors to the world . . . and how to turn it off when the electronic noise gets too loud.

★ CAPTAIN VIDEO ★

It's not unusual for preschool kids to spend more time with TV than with their grand-parents. Most of them know more ad jingles than songs. On most days kids will meet more television characters than real people. TV is a big source of spoken and written language, and it has a powerful voice. Experts suggest that it's a good idea to put limits on what kind of and how much TV and video your child watches. Here are some TV guidelines that work for some real kids in some real households. See if they work in yours.

MAKE TV RULES

- Write the rules down together, even if your kid doesn't read. Refer to them.
- Make a per day TV limit. Let your children pick their shows (subject to your approval).
- Turn it off after the show is over. Don't let it spill into other shows or activities.
- Declare one day a week a No-TV Day. Make this a rule that everyone sticks to.

When the TV goes off you might suggest an alternate activity, but some parents prefer to let kids invent their own things to do. Despite the moans, they'll come up with something.

TV TICKETS

Around the first grade you might have success with a ticket system. Give your child a week's worth of TV tickets. At our house this equals 12 half-hours of TV. Tickets left over at the end of the week are redeemable for money, for instance 25 cents. (No, you can't use them next week.) Expensive, but worth it!

WATCHING

- Watch each show with your kid at least once. Talk about it afterward. Evaluate how your little one reacts. Even though a program is supposed to be for children it might be too scary for your child.
- Consider taping adult shows for you to view later. This can keep your kids from overhearing a lot of TV programs you wish they didn't.

> It's your turn to *die*, you no-good, miserable, wife-stealer! ⁼ BANG! ⁼

RENTING MOVIES

- If it's PG, it's a video that is too sophisticated for your preschooler.
- Kids vary. What is disturbing for one four-year-old may be fine for another. Be on the alert and flip off the tube if you notice your child becoming uneasy.
- Allow your child to control the TV, not be controlled by it. When a video gets scary, encourage your kid to leave the room and to take a peek when she's ready.
- Make a Scaredy Cat. "If kitty gets scared during the show, bring him to me."

MAKE TV ACTIVE. A major drawback to TV is that it turns watchers into zombies. Try anything to make TV more active for your child:

- Have her color or draw while watching.
- Use TV as a conversation starter. "Tell me three things that happened on 'Sesame Street' today."
- Invite your child's dolls and bears to watch the show. Ask your kid what she thought about the program.
- Talk back to the TV. Ask, "Do you believe that?" Be skeptical. Suggest other views. "Our dog hates that kind of food."

PRIME TIME KIT. Fill a shoe box with materials for alternate activities. Pull it out when you're busy and tempted to use the TV as a babysitter. It might include:

★ PLUGGED IN PLAY ★

Electronic things have the power to really grab a kid's interest. Little ones love the buttons, beeps, and squeaks of electronic gizmos. Computer games and battery-powered toys can make a rich addition to the world of learning and play, but they need to be thoughtfully designed. Here are some criteria.

COMPUTER GAMES. Your child does not need a computer in his or her life. If you do have one and you don't mind allowing your child to use it, computers can be rewarding fun for little ones. They do have many things to recommend them over TV. Computers are:

- Active. TV is passive. You must do something to a computer to make it respond.
- Infinitely patient.
- Challenging. While their puzzling aspects can make them infuriating, computers offer a lot of problem-solving practice.
- Fascinating for kids. Their sounds, color, and animation allow them to combine learning and play in an enjoyable way.

CHOOSING. The same criteria apply to computer games as well as any handheld electronic learning toys. Good ones are:

- Easy to use, with clear directions.
- Age-appropriate and have a range of skill levels for longer life.
- Under the child's control. The program lets the kid choose what to do.
- Full of fantasy and fun.
- Applicable to the real world. (Learning letters, for example, not shooting flying hamburgers with mustard guns.)
- Open-ended. They encourage exploring and creating. Avoid programs that seem like workbooks with bells and whistles.

SUGGESTIONS: Computer programs change fast, so talk with a knowledgeable dealer about the best children's software. Test programs and toys first, if possible.

★ TALKING ON TAPE ★

Kids love playing with tape recorders. Recording has the magical quality of giving kids instant feedback. Tape recorders are wonderful tools for getting children to really listen to themselves and others. They are an open invitation to play with words . . . in all sorts of interesting ways.

INTERVIEW. Sometimes the most chatterbox kids suddenly forget they know how to talk when faced with a recorder (don't we all?). Help your child forget her shyness by playing the reporter. Try an interview:

HINT: Some kids, especially four- and five-year-olds, might do better talking and running the recorder themselves.

JUST TALK. Tape recorders can give kids the sense that what they have to say is important and worth recording. And it is! How kids talk changes and changes fast. It's great fun to keep some tapes so you can remember how Jean sounded when she was three.

HOLIDAY TALES. At the end of a wild holiday, recount what happened. Who did you see? What did you eat? Where did you go? Send the tape to Grandma. She can add it to her tape library of favorite kid-made stories and songs.

LET'S TELL the story of the birthday when you turned six. How did the day start? What did you wear? What was the best thing that happened? What was the worst? Now say good night!

AUTOMATIC STORIES. Some parents like to read a favorite story on tape. They ring a bell when it's time for a page turn. The child can read along while listening, even when the parent is not present.

★ INDEX ★

Use this index to quickly find an appropriate activity for whatever circumstances you and your preschooler happen to be in. Check the Table of Contents at the front of this book for a complete activity list.